Safely Through the Storm

DAN QUELLO

HARVEST HOUSE PUBLISHERS
Eugene, Oregon 97402

Illustrations by Lynda Adkins

SAFELY THROUGH THE STORM

Copyright © 1992 by Harvest House Publishers
Eugene, Oregon 97402

Library of Congress Cataloging-in-Publication Data

Quello, Dan, 1941-
    Safely through the storm / Dan Quello.
    Summary: Compares a child's growth toward maturity to a voyage at sea, and divorce to a storm the family has encountered.
    ISBN 0-89081-860-6
    1. Children of divorced parents—United States—Juvenile literature.
    2. Divorce—United States—Juvenile literature.   [1. Divorce.]
    I. Title.
    HQ777.5.Q45   1992
    306.89—dc20   92-11410
                                                                                                CIP
                                                                                                AC

All rights reserved. No portion of this book may be reproduced in any form without the written permission of the Publisher.

Printed in the United States of America.

This book is about growing up at a time when your parents are growing apart.

By comparing your life to a voyage at sea and your parents' divorce to a storm, this book will help you make it "Safely Through the Storm"!

Contents

 1. Bon Voyage! 7
 2. Welcome Aboard! 9
 3. Charting a Course 11
 4. Calm Before the Storm 13
 5. Sea Squalls 15
 6. Gale Warnings 17
 7. Hoping the Storm Will Pass 19
 8. Who Rocked the Boat? 21
 9. On the Rocks 23
10. Different Moorings 25
11. Do You Read Me? 27
12. S.O.S (Save Our Ship) 29
13. Your North Star 31
14. Setting Your Sail 33
15. The Deep Water 35
16. All Hands on Deck! 37
17. A Tight Ship 39
18. A New First Mate 41
19. Keeping a Logbook 43
20. Regattas and Other Special Events 45
21. Looking for Rainbows 47
22. Seasoned Sailors 49
23. Harbor Lights 51

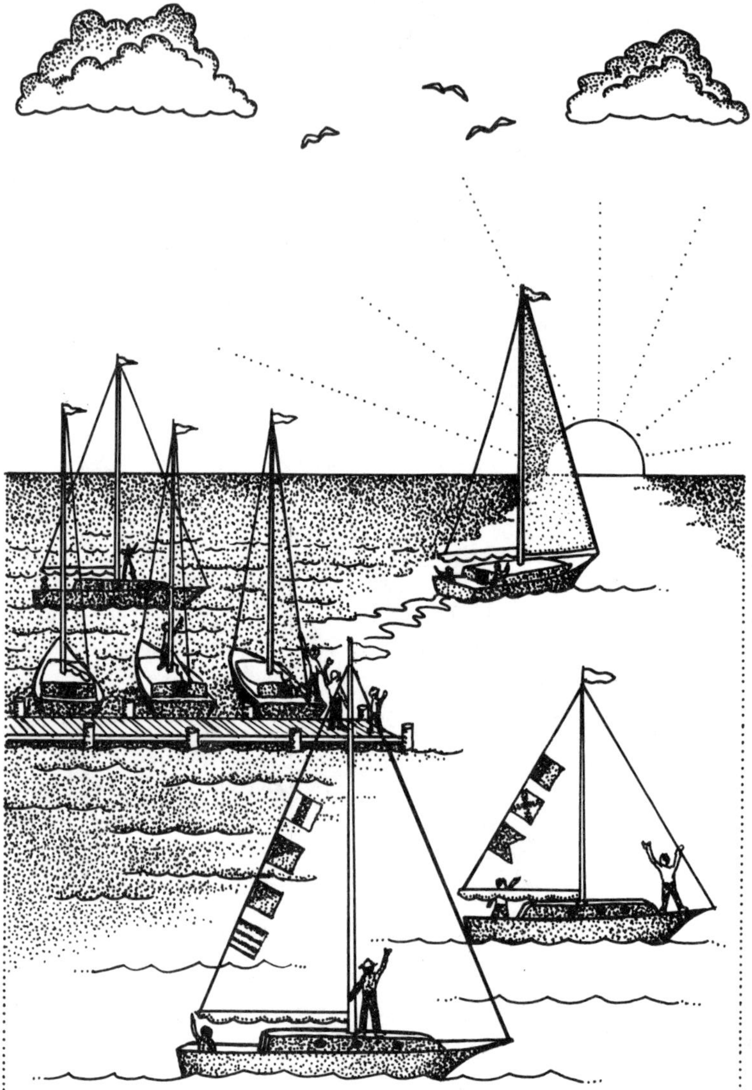

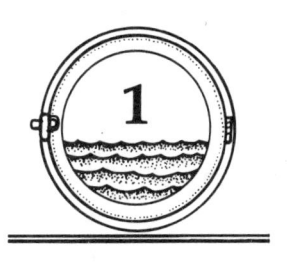

Bon Voyage!

*I*magine a world in which all people who marry live their lives at sea. This would mean that the day your parents were married was the beginning of a very important voyage.

Grandparents, neighbors, and friends all gathered around to wish them their best. Because they had chosen each other for this voyage, their wedding day was a happy and wonderful time.

Bravely, confidently, and filled with high hopes... they set sail!

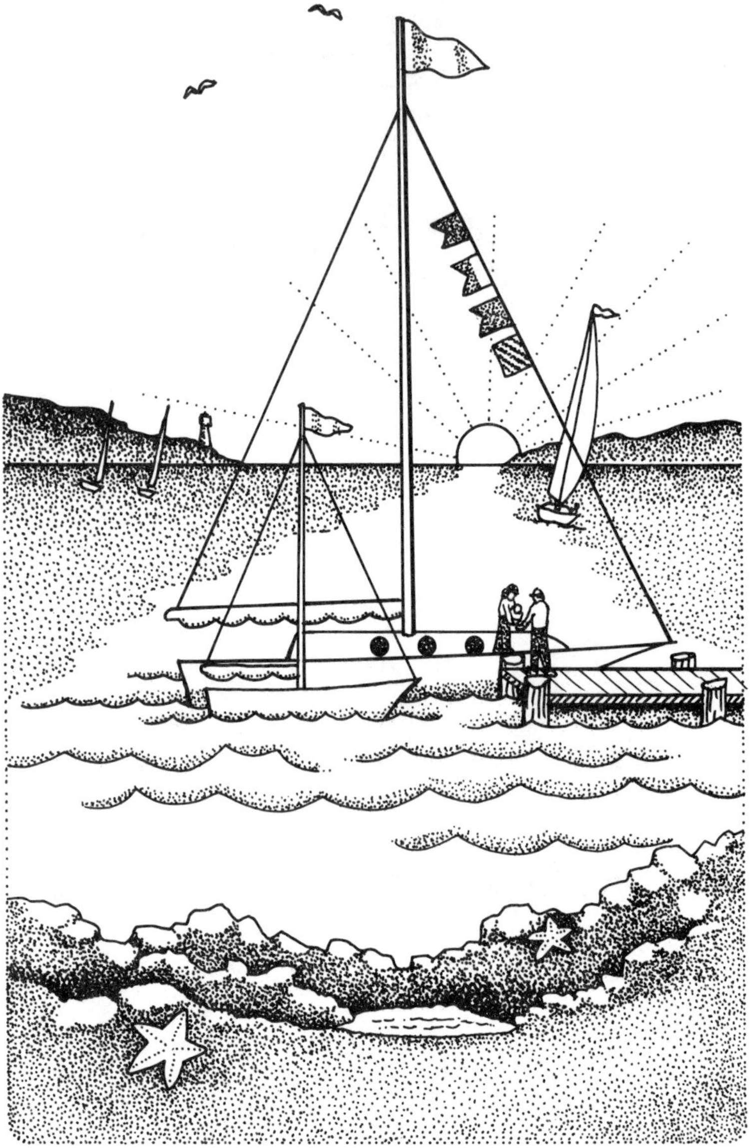

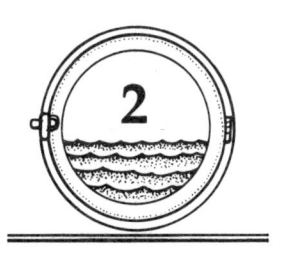

Welcome Aboard!

*I*t must have been a happy day when your father and mother welcomed you aboard.

A little bit of Dad... a little bit of Mom... and yet a totally new person. Your arrival brought them much delight!

Friends from neighboring boats joined in the celebration, letting your parents and you know that it was good that you were here.

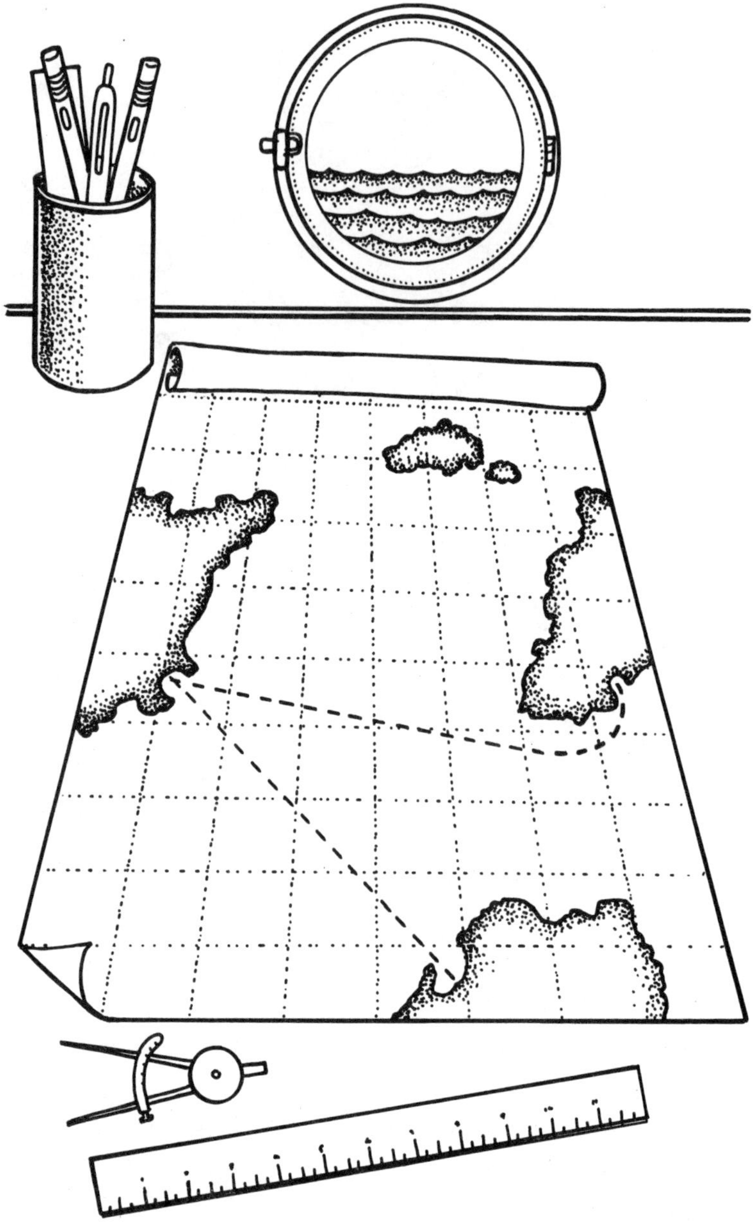

Charting a Course

At the start of a voyage, it's a good idea to know where you are going and how you are going to get there. Because storms sometimes arise at sea, you may have to alter your course, but your destination usually remains unchanged.

In your family's voyage, ever since you were born it has been your parents' desire to help you reach the shores of young adulthood. Just how you get there may depend upon the storms you encounter, but your safe passage from childhood to adulthood will always be important to each parent.

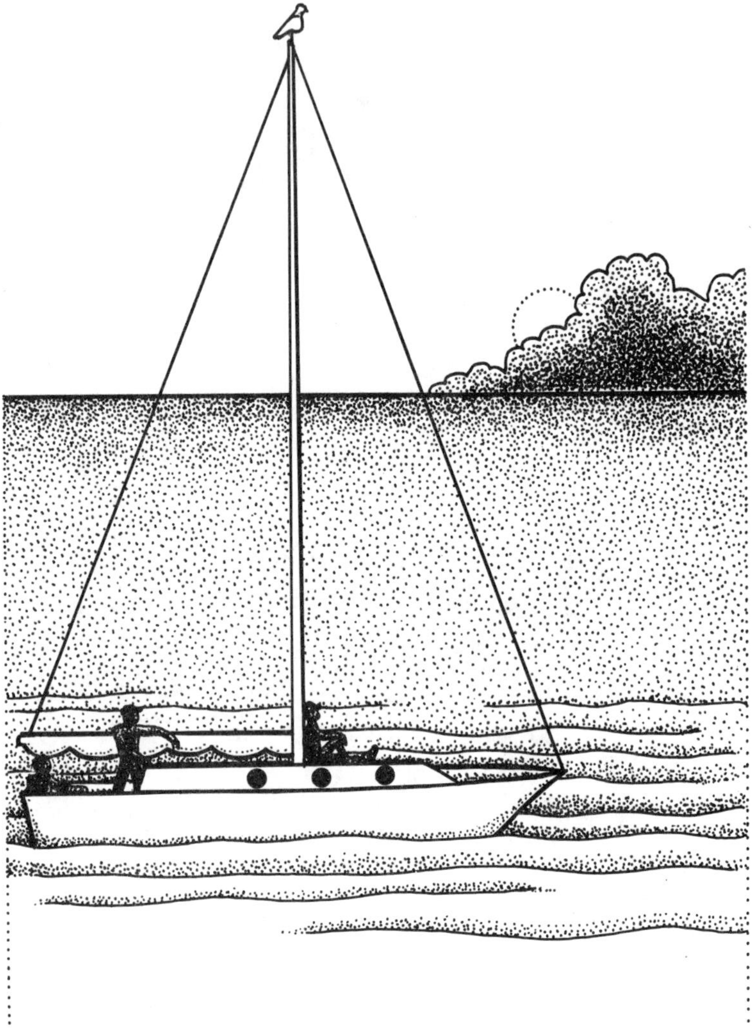

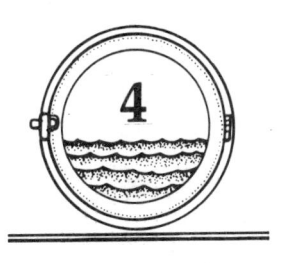

Calm Before the Storm

People who live at sea sometimes speak of a calm before the storm. Some children experience a similar calm before their parents announce their decision to divorce.

On the surface, Mom and Dad seem to be getting along fine. The family's needs are being met, and everyone appears to be happy, at least most of the time.

Many children are unaware of their parents' unhappiness before they decide to divorce.

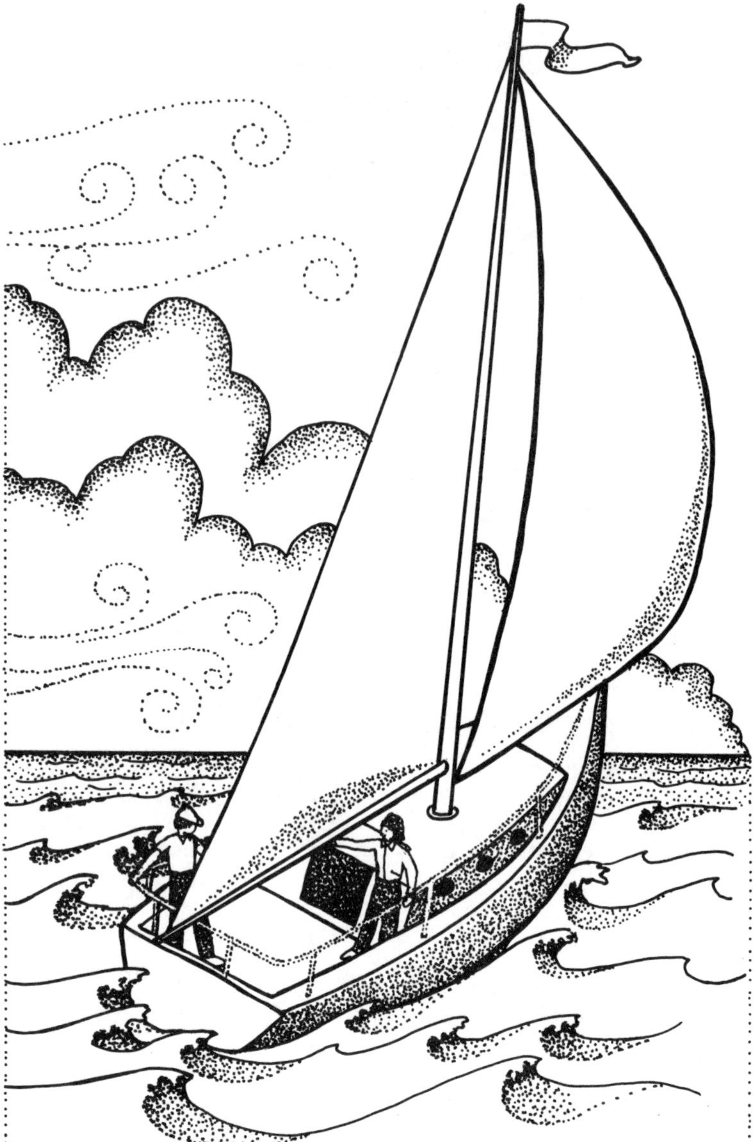

Sea Squalls

A squall is a sudden and often violent windstorm that arises at sea.

Some parents' decision to divorce sweeps upon their children like a squall. Out of an angry quarrel, a broken promise, or a major disappointment may come the decision to divorce.

When a parent is feeling angry or sad about the divorce it may be hard for him or her to talk with you about it. When he or she is able to tell you, however, you will want to know where you will be living, how often you will be seeing each parent, and the reasons for their divorce. You don't have to know every detail, but you'll be better able to accept the divorce if you have a general sense of what your parents' problems are.

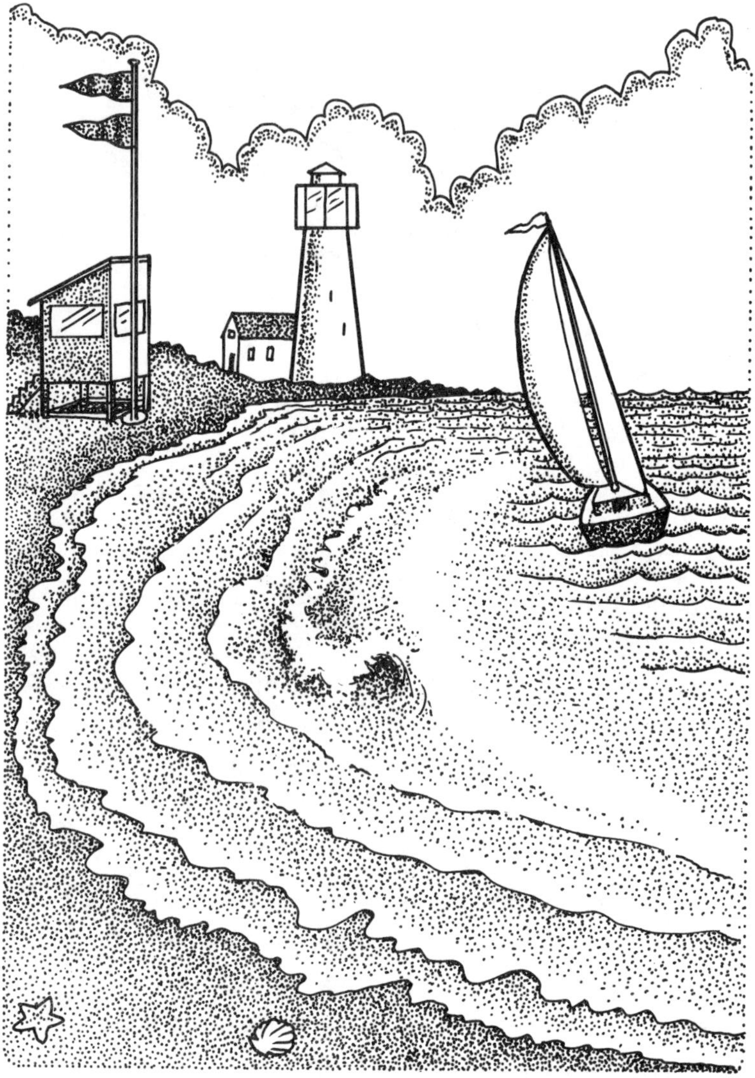

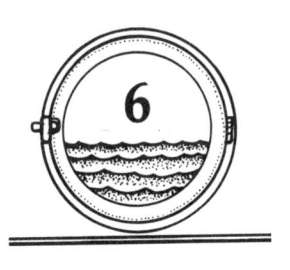

Gale Warnings

Some children have months, even years, to prepare for their parents' divorce. The constant fighting, shouting, and tears are like gale warnings to the children of some households.

If your parents' divorce has come about in this way, it is still very sad, but at least you are somewhat prepared for it.

If your parents' fighting has made it difficult for you to have friends over and hard to study, or has even kept you awake at night, your parents' divorce may bring peaceful changes to your home.

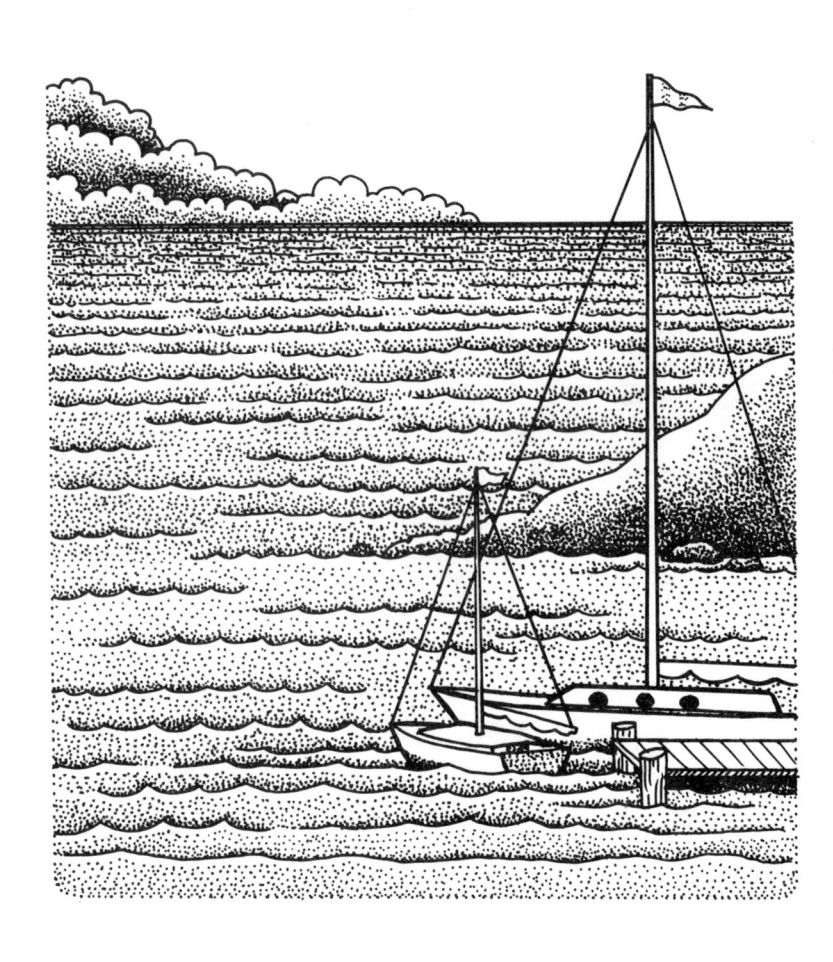

Hoping the Storm Will Pass

*I*f you are like most children, you do not want your parents to get divorced. You love each of them and they love you. You wonder why they can't love each other.

Perhaps you have begged them to stay together. You may even have cried yourself to sleep, hoping that this storm would pass. Very likely your parents will not marry each other again, but your feelings about them and yourself will get better!

Children whose parents have been divorced for some time say that while they had trouble accepting their parents' divorce at the time, now, two or three years later, most of them have learned to accept it and still feel close to both parents.

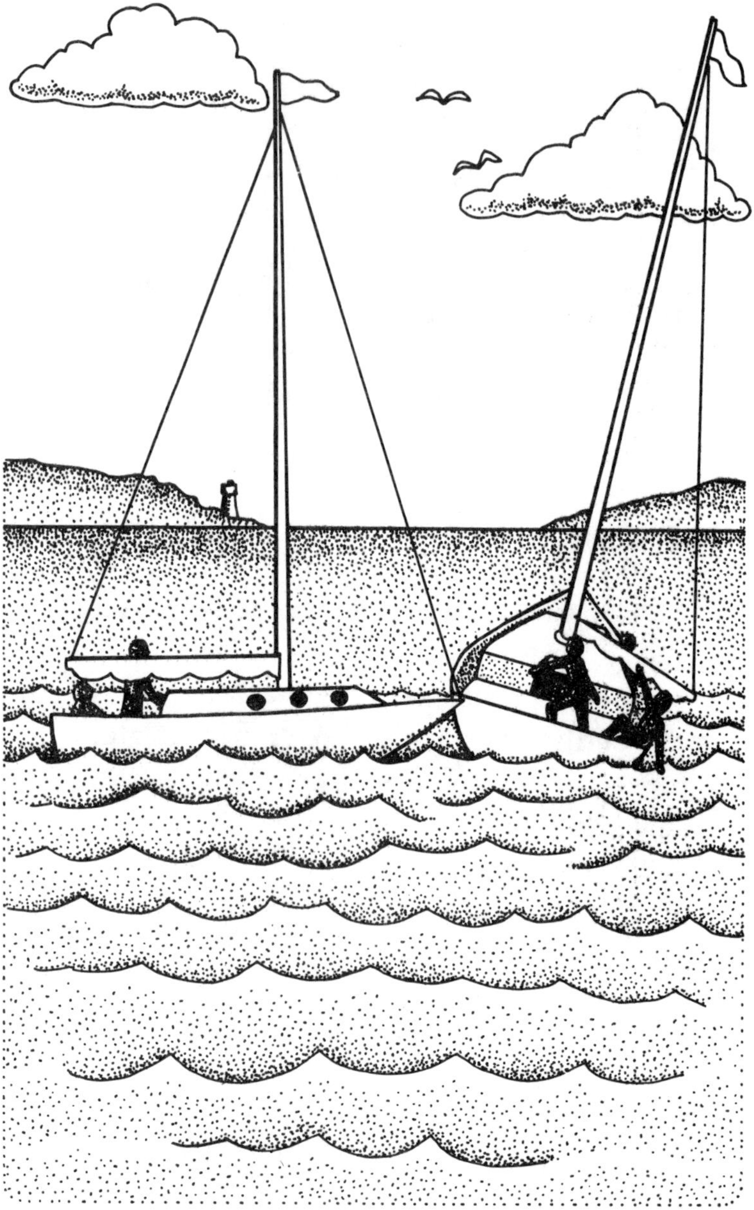

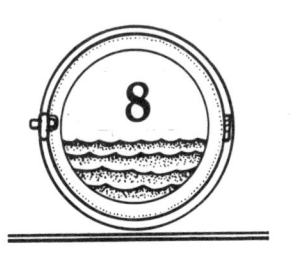

Who Rocked the Boat?

Many children would like to know who rocked the boat. It's not that you are looking for someone to blame, it's just that you feel you could better accept your parents' divorce if you understood the reasons for it.

Your parents may or may not be able to answer all your questions. Some parents tend to blame the other. Others are careful not to blame anyone. Still others have reasons so complicated that they themselves don't fully understand them.

One thing you should be very clear about: Children are never to blame for their parents' divorce.

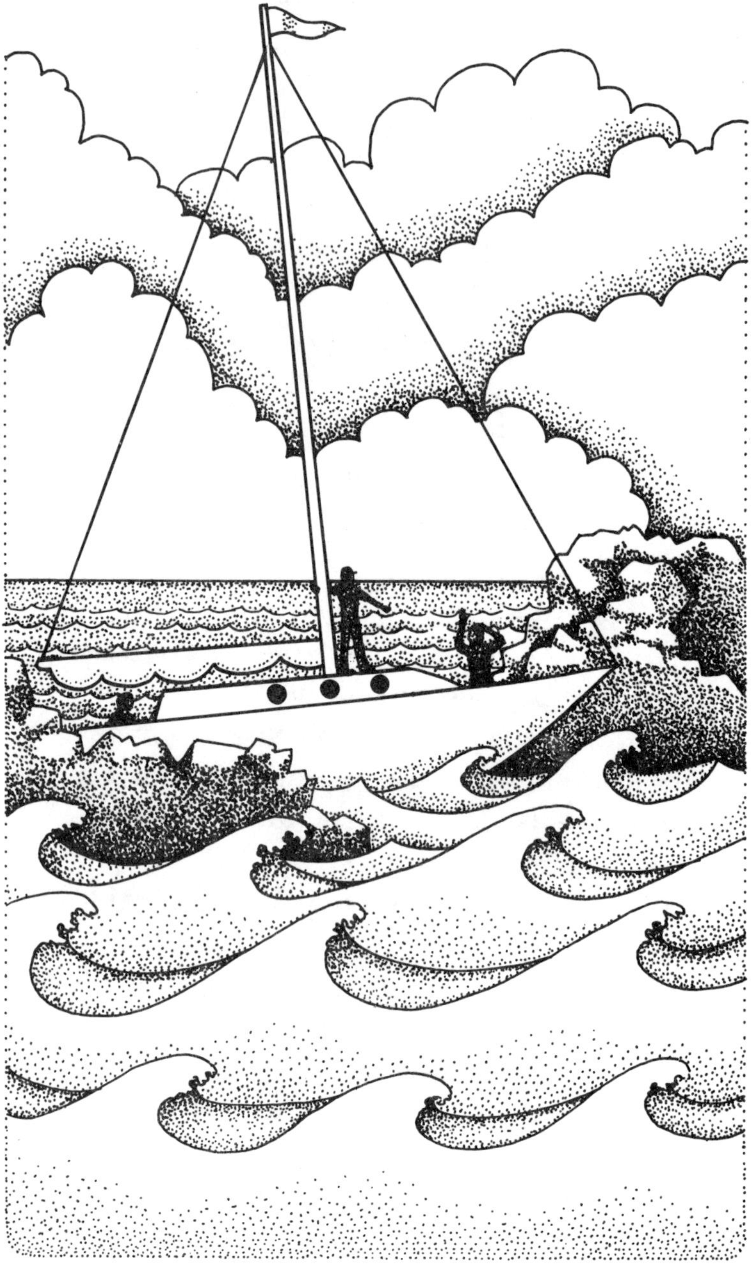

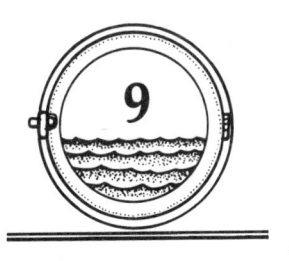

On the Rocks

*J*ust as every boat encounters its storms, so every family has its hard times.

Some families seem able to ride out the storms. Some are even drawn more closely together because of the storms. But others find storms to be their undoing. Even a very good boat can be tossed upon the rocks in a storm.

If your parents' marriage is on the rocks, it is important to remember that the divorce is between *them*, not between *you and them*! Your love for each of them and their love for you is unchanged. Getting to where you want to go can still be accomplished, except that now you will spend some time aboard two boats instead of one.

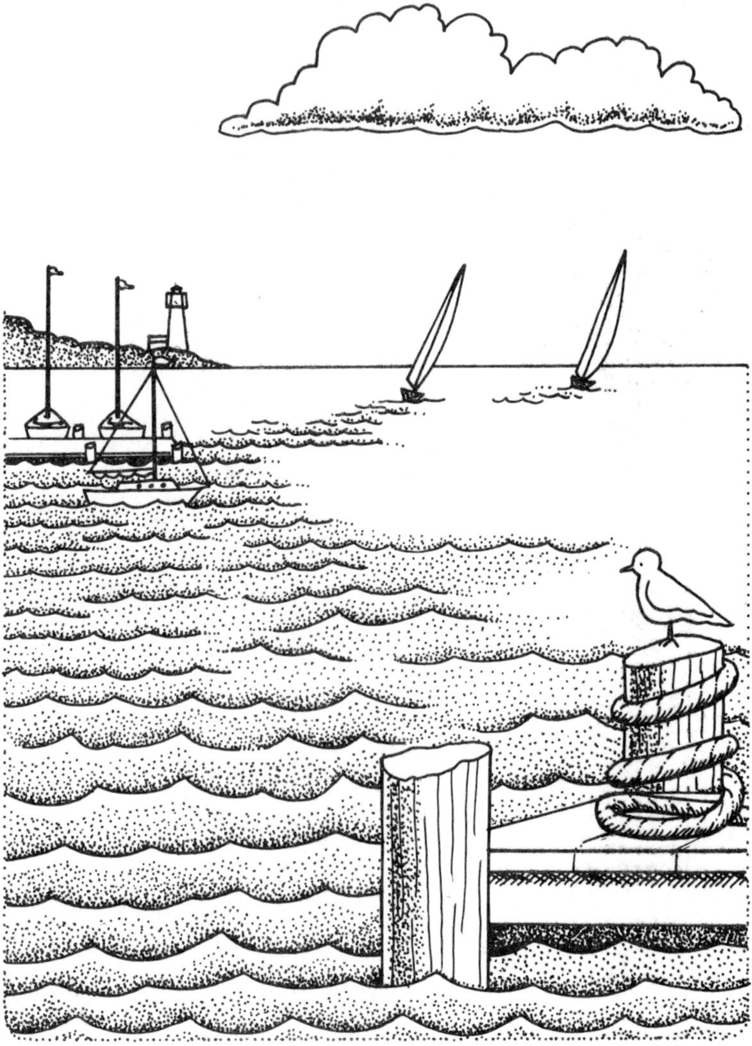

10

Different Moorings

Living aboard two boats can be fun... it can also be difficult. Since your parents no longer live together, you will probably spend some time living with each.

There may be times when you are at one parent's home and you wish you could be with friends or doing activities at the other. You might decide to go snorkeling, only to discover that your mask and fins are at the other house.

But there is a bright side too! Living in two different households, in two different neighborhoods, can mean twice as many things to see and do. With a little imagination you can discover something to do, someone to help, or some activity to enjoy in each place.

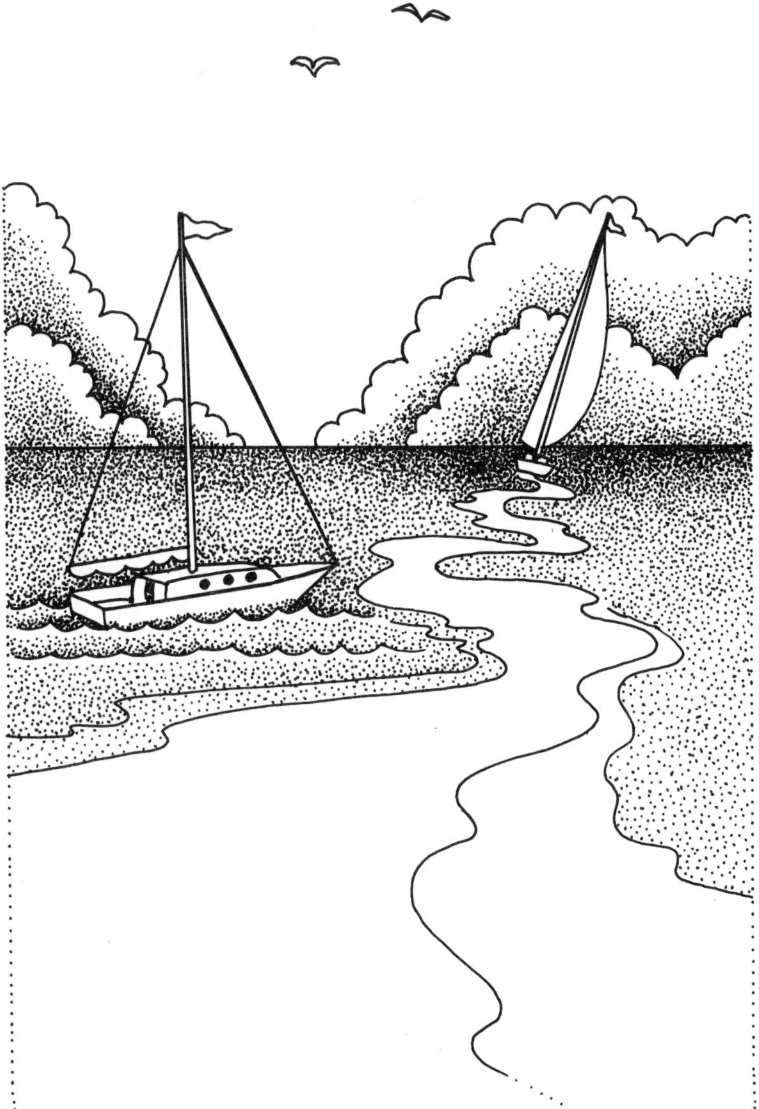

Do You Read Me?

No matter how much love you have for each parent, there will be times when you have other feelings as well. Feelings of anger, disappointment, and betrayal are all very common.

Some children think it is wrong to have bad feelings toward their mother or father. They think they should feel love all the time.

It might help you to know that all children get angry at their parents at times... especially when there has been a divorce. When you have feelings you don't understand, or would rather not have, remember that it's only natural to have these feelings, and even to express them. But try to do so with respect.

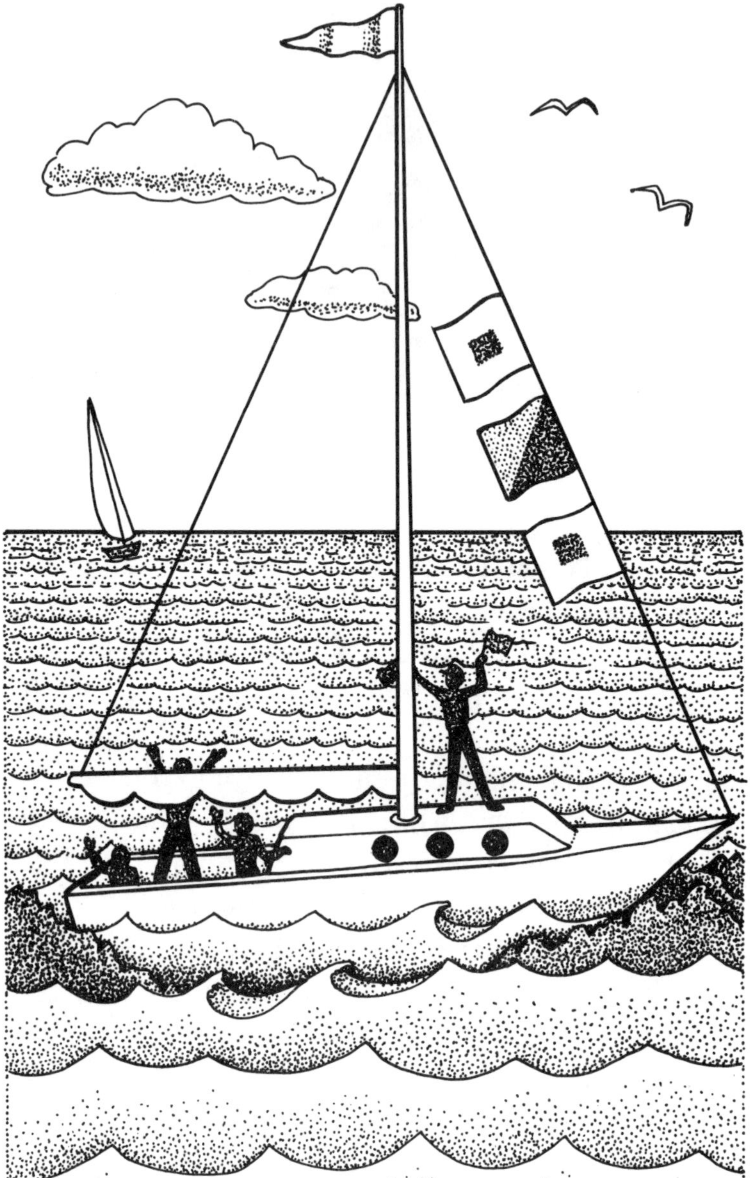

S.O.S (Save Our Ship)

*I*n times of distress boaters often send out an S.O.S. That's a universal call for help. When a family is struggling to stay afloat, it is not uncommon for parents or children to send out an S.O.S. Fortunately, there are many people who will hear and respond to your call.

The feeling you may have during your parents' divorce is, "I'm all alone in this." You'll feel much better if you can talk with someone else about it. You may choose to talk with a school counselor, pastor, grandparent, or neighborhood friend for the help and understanding you need. Often, someone who has been through an experience like yours can be the most helpful.

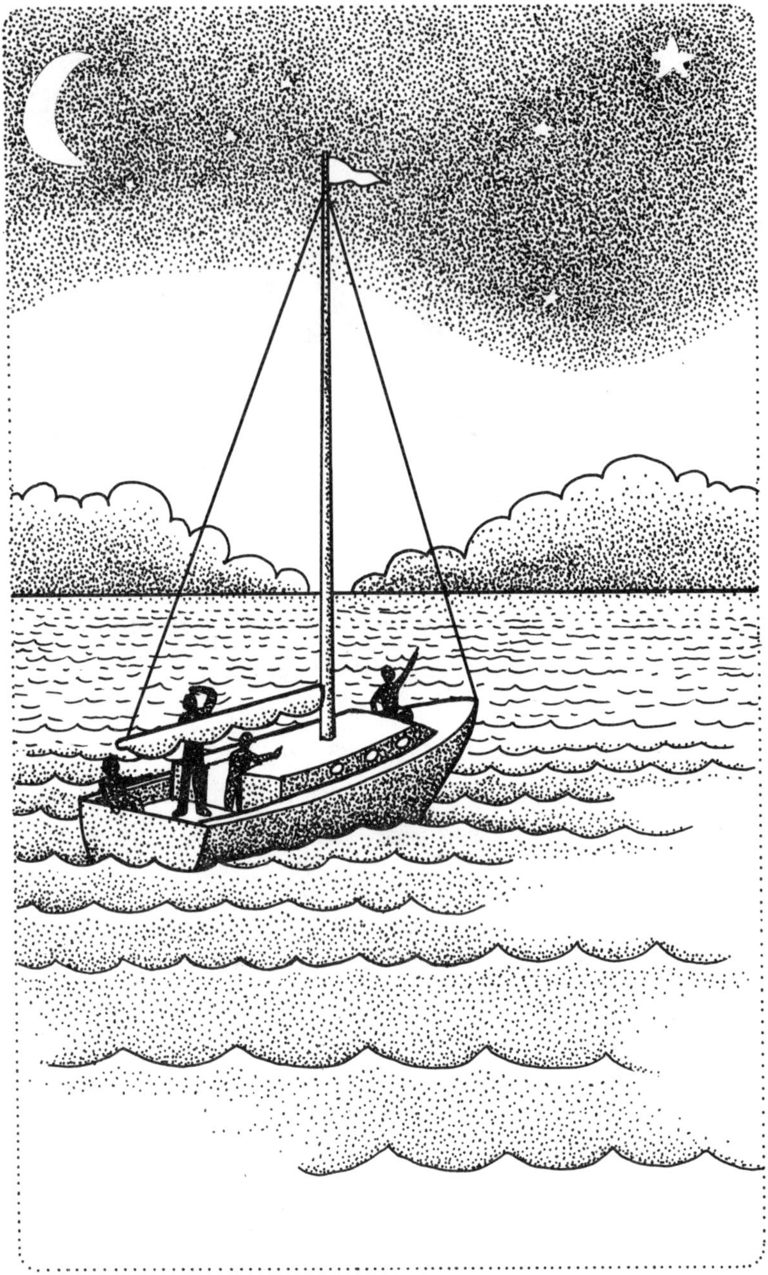

Your North Star

When sailors feel lost at sea, they often look into the heavens for the North Star. Getting a line on the North Star helps them find their bearings at sea.

Young people who feel tossed about in the troubled waters of divorce often turn to God for answers. It's good to know that the God who gave you life has promised to be with you in good times and in bad.

People who turn to God for comfort, hope, and direction find it. You may choose to think of God as your Guiding Light.

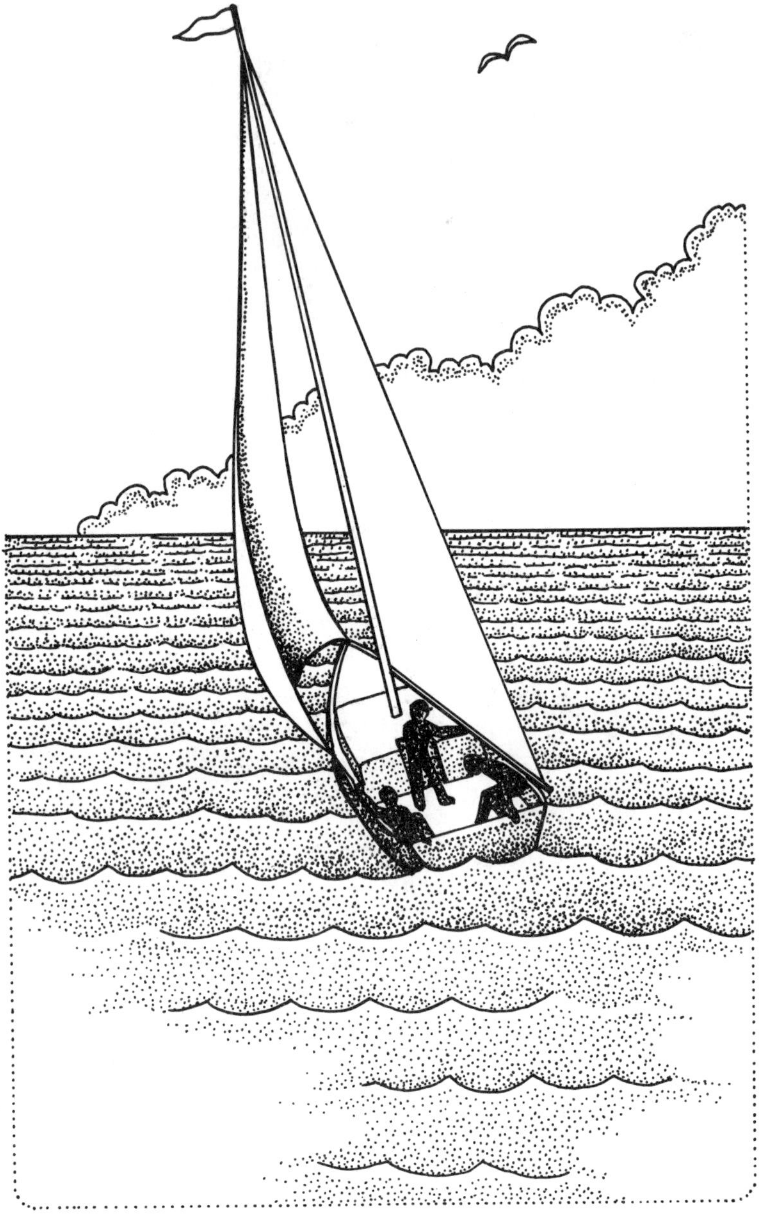

Setting Your Sail

A wise sailor once said, "You can't control the gale, but you can set your sail." There are many things in life which you cannot control. Your parents' decision to get a divorce is one of them.

Although you may feel helpless to do anything about it, you are not. You can choose the way you will deal with the changes brought on by the divorce.

By so doing, you will be like the wise sailor who chooses the set for his sail, angles his boat into the wind, and makes progress even against the storm.

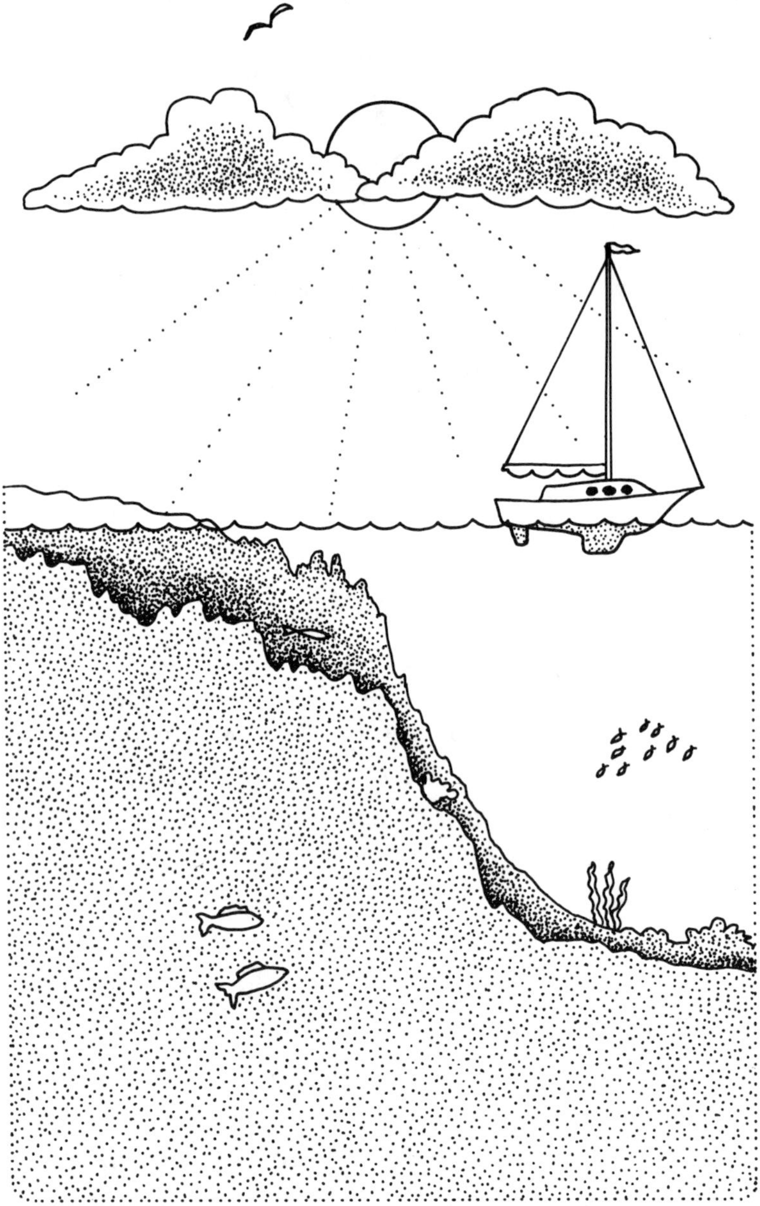

The Deep Water

You need not know every rock or sandbar in the waters of divorce to continue safely on your voyage. All you need to know is where the water runs deep. The deep water in most families is the love that parents and children have for each other.

Feelings of anger, blame, and rejection may be like rocks or sandbars lying hidden beneath the surface. You may bump into them from time to time, but to keep from getting hung up, you will want to continue your voyages in the deep water of your love for each parent and their love for you.

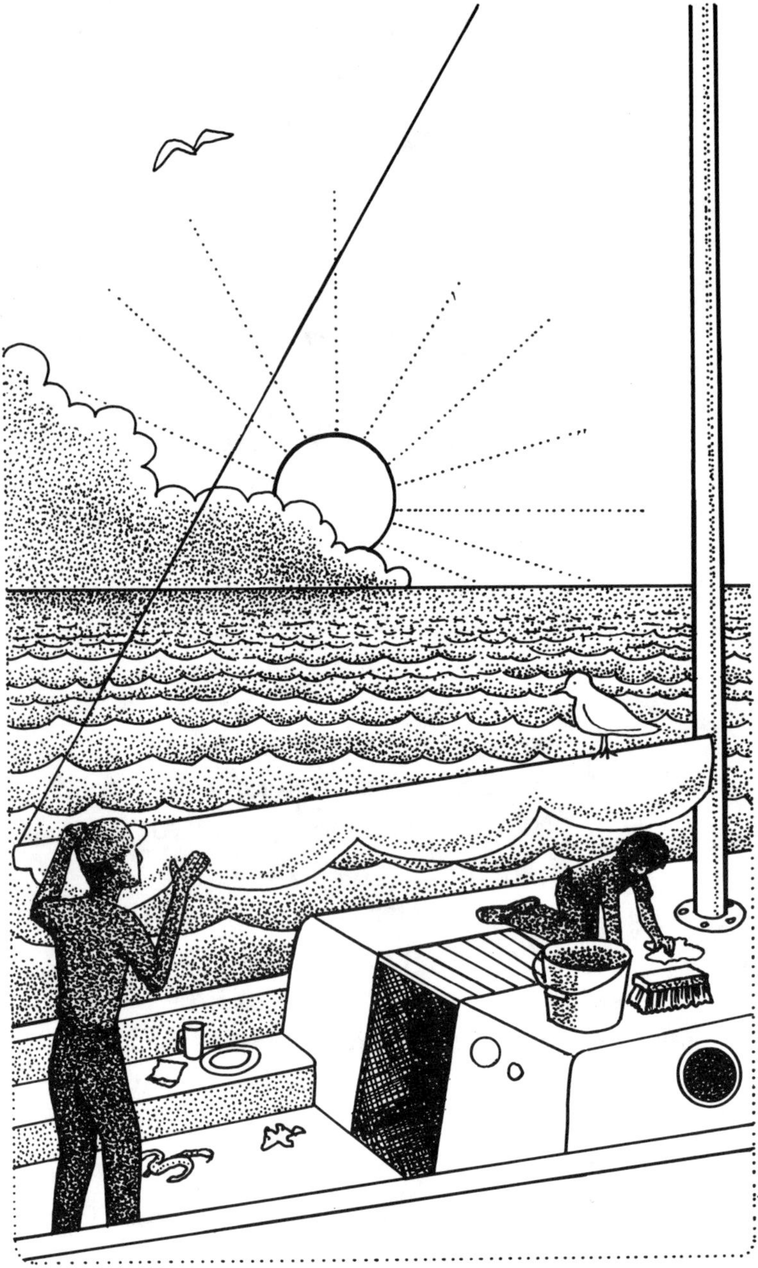

All Hands on Deck!

A successful voyage depends upon the willingness of each crew member to do his or her job well.

Since the divorce of your parents, there are now two households to maintain. That may mean that each parent now has fewer hours available for you. It may also mean that each parent now needs your help more than ever before.

Cleaning the house, making your own lunch, and putting yourself to bed may be some of the ways you can help each parent through this difficult stretch of the voyage.

Perhaps even before the call goes out for "all hands on deck" you can make a parent's day by volunteering your services.

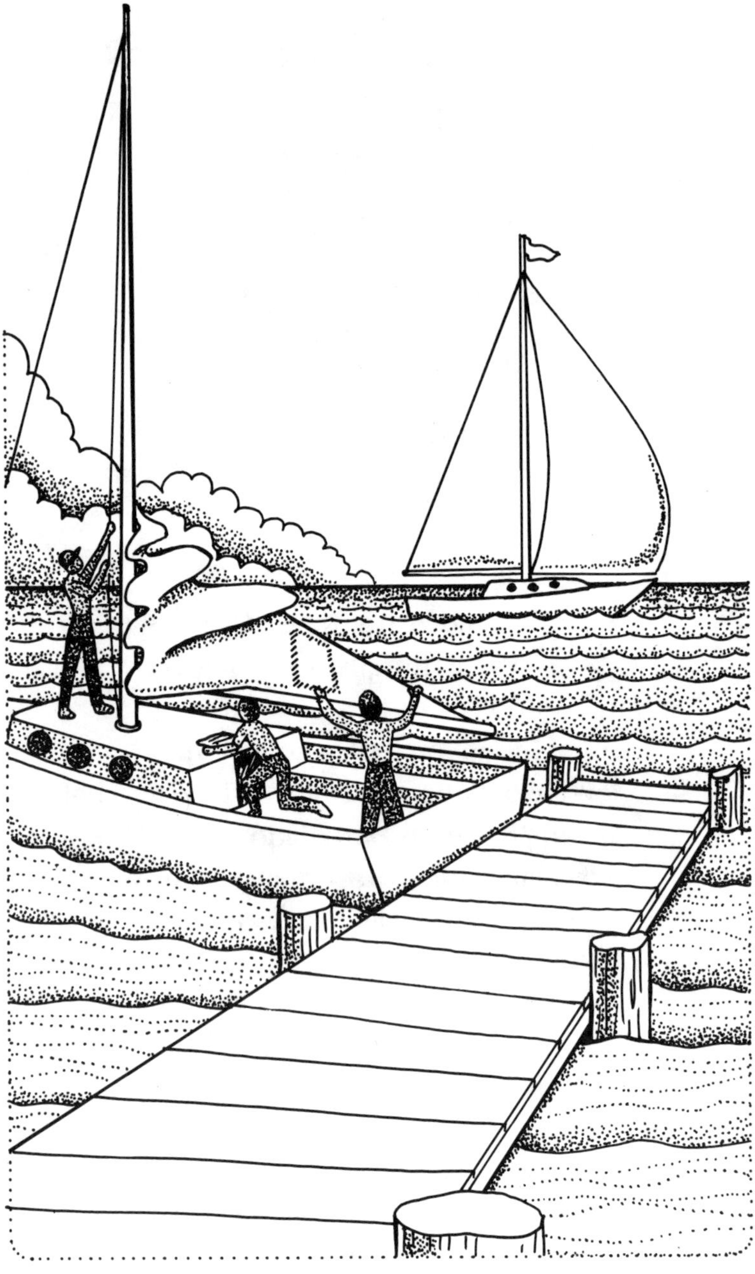

A Tight Ship

*I*t takes money to run a ship. It takes even more to run two ships! Because the money available to your parents before their divorce must now be used to run two households, there will generally be less of it to go around. This may change in time, but for now you may have to learn to get along on less!

Running a tight ship can be a good experience. You will discover that you can get along on less when you have to. With less to spend you will learn to be more careful how you spend it. And perhaps you will see that people and friendships are more important than things!

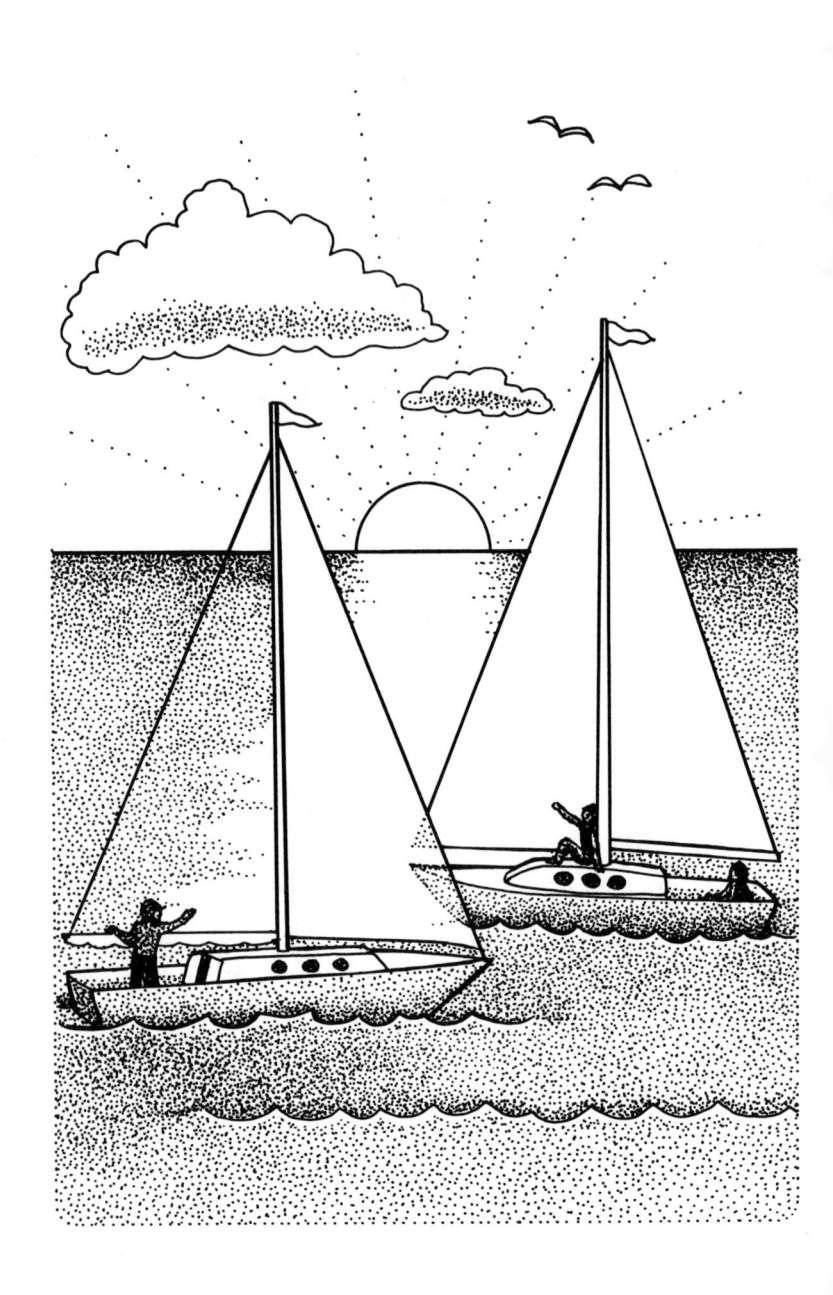

A New First Mate

Nobody can take the place of your own mother or father, nor would anybody want to. Yet a time may come when your father or mother welcomes someone new into his or her life. It might seem strange to you at first to see a parent with someone else. You could feel embarrassed or even betrayed when one of them begins to date.

You may be helped in overcoming these feelings by knowing that divorce is a legal way of saying the marriage is over, and each parent is now free to start over.

It may take some time to get used to your mom or dad loving another person. Yet, the happier your parents are, the better parents they will be to you!

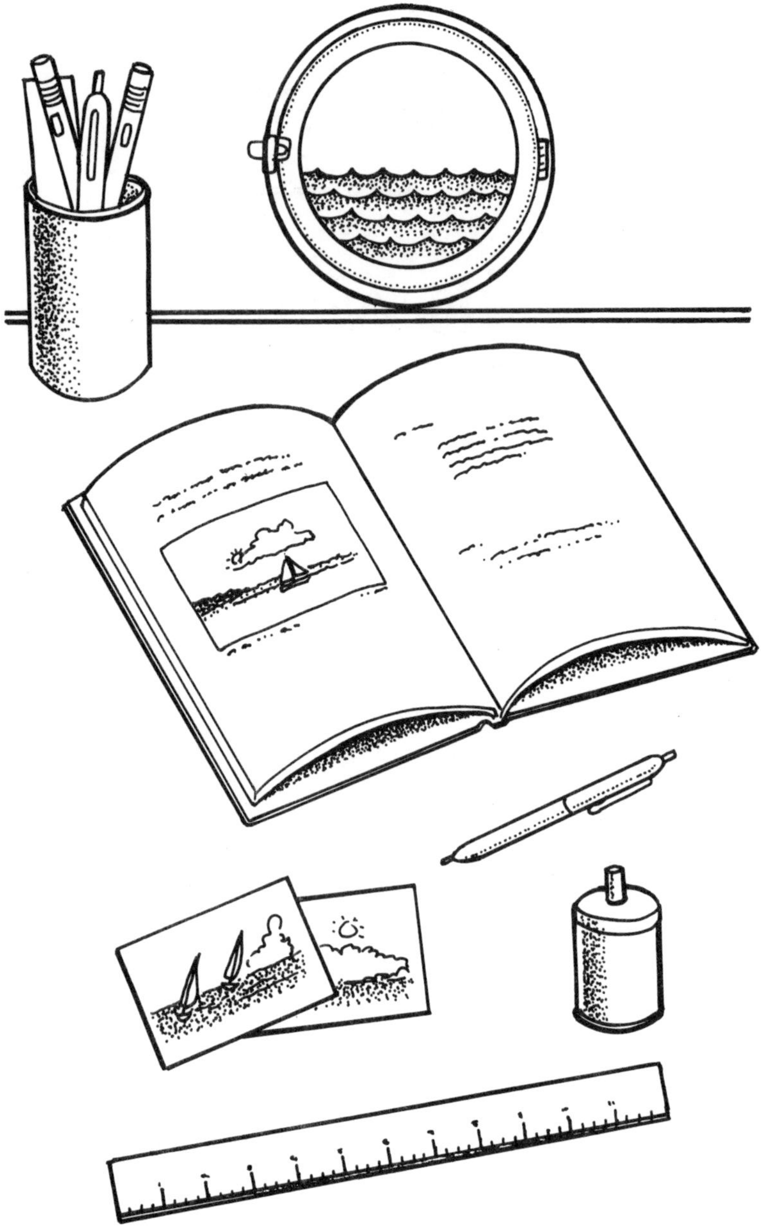

Keeping A Logbook

*I*t is not uncommon to miss one parent while off doing something special with the other. It's easy to wish that the other parent was there enjoying the experience with you.

A good way to share those experiences with the non-present parent is to take pictures and keep a logbook. Keeping a logbook will also help you remember special places and times with each parent.

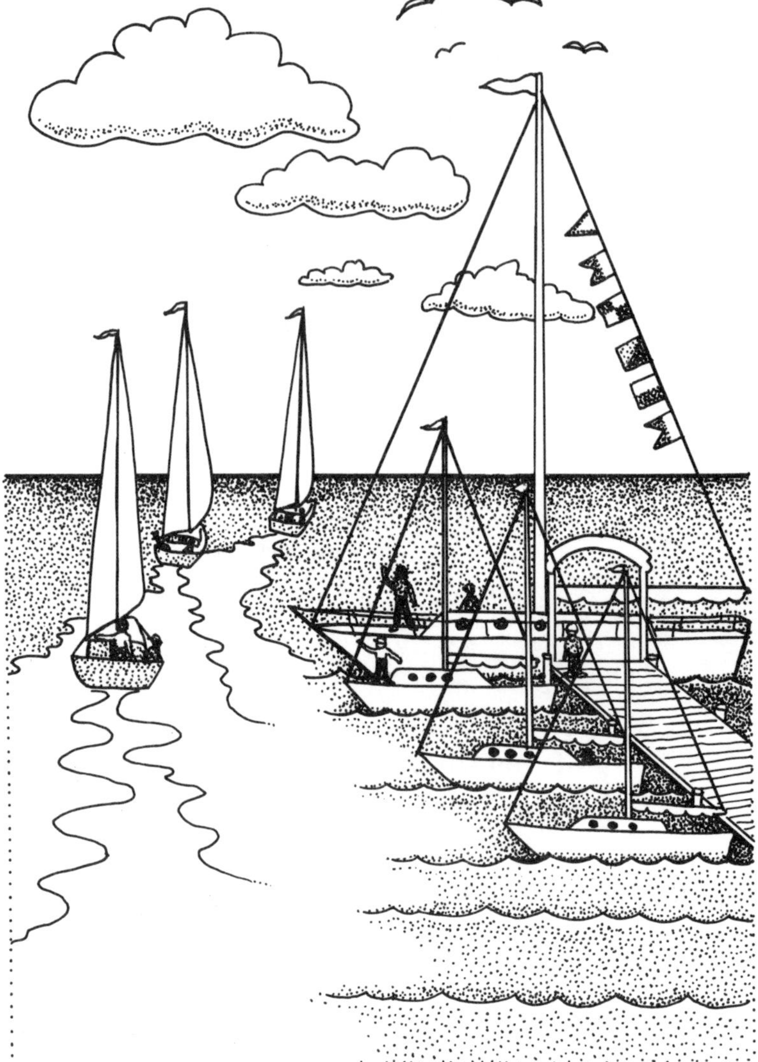

Regattas and Other Special Events

Everyone loves a regatta. Boats and crews from all around come together on race days. There are special times like that for families too. Weddings, birthdays, baptisms, and graduations... all have a way of bringing people together.

Your parents' divorce may cause you to feel uncomfortable at some of these gatherings. Just wondering who to sit with, or how much time to spend visiting with each parent, may be a problem. You may even wonder if it's all right to show affection to one parent in the presence of the other.

As much as possible, try not to let your parents' feelings about each other stand in the way of your love for each of them. Neither of them will love you less because of your love for the other.

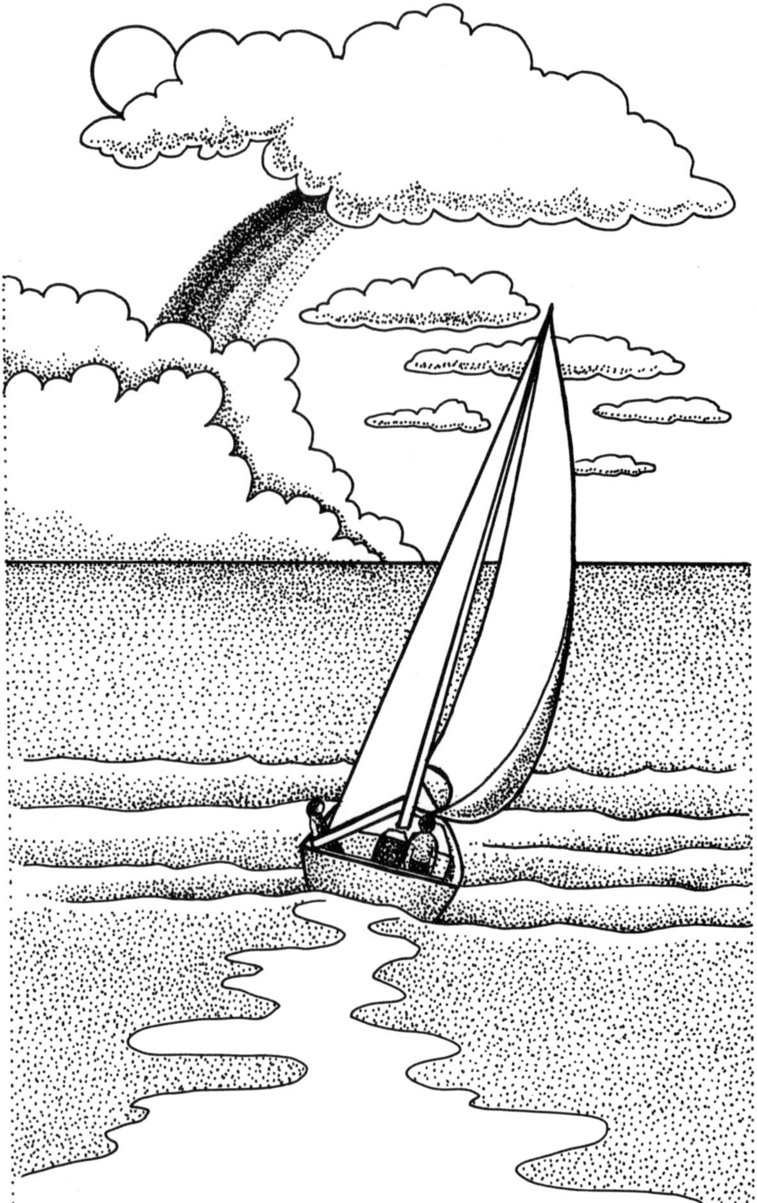

Looking for Rainbows

*A*s you move through a storm, be on the watch for rainbows. Rainbows often signal the end of a storm. The sun's rays shining through the last drops of rain create an arc of color signaling brighter days ahead.

One of the most important things to remember about any storm is that one day it will end. As you and your family settle into new ways of doing things, you may discover a rainbow of happiness right where you are!

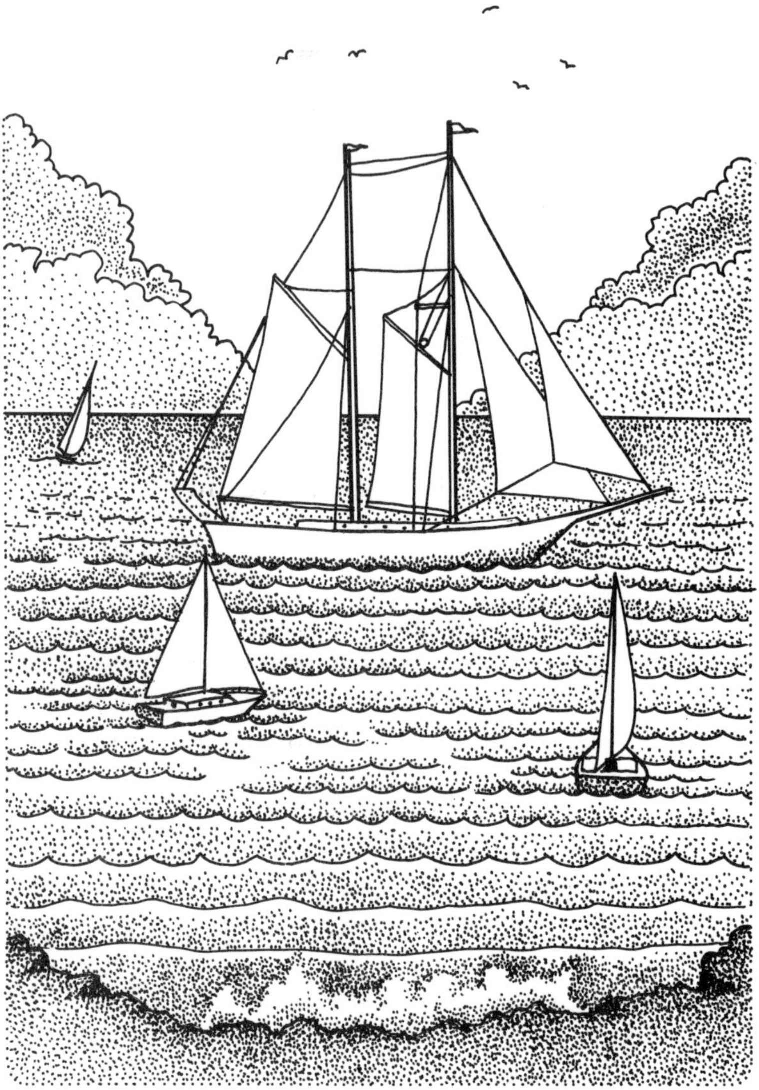

Seasoned Sailors

Only when you've weathered a few storms can you be called a seasoned sailor. Quite likely your parents' divorce has meant some difficult sailing for both you and them. Yet these same experiences have helped you to grow.

Perhaps even more than children from homes with two parents, you have learned how to keep your balance in a storm. Your experiences have made you better able to manage yourself. Added responsibilities have increased your confidence and given you a pride in accomplishment. Because of what you have been through, you may also be more sensitive to other people and their needs.

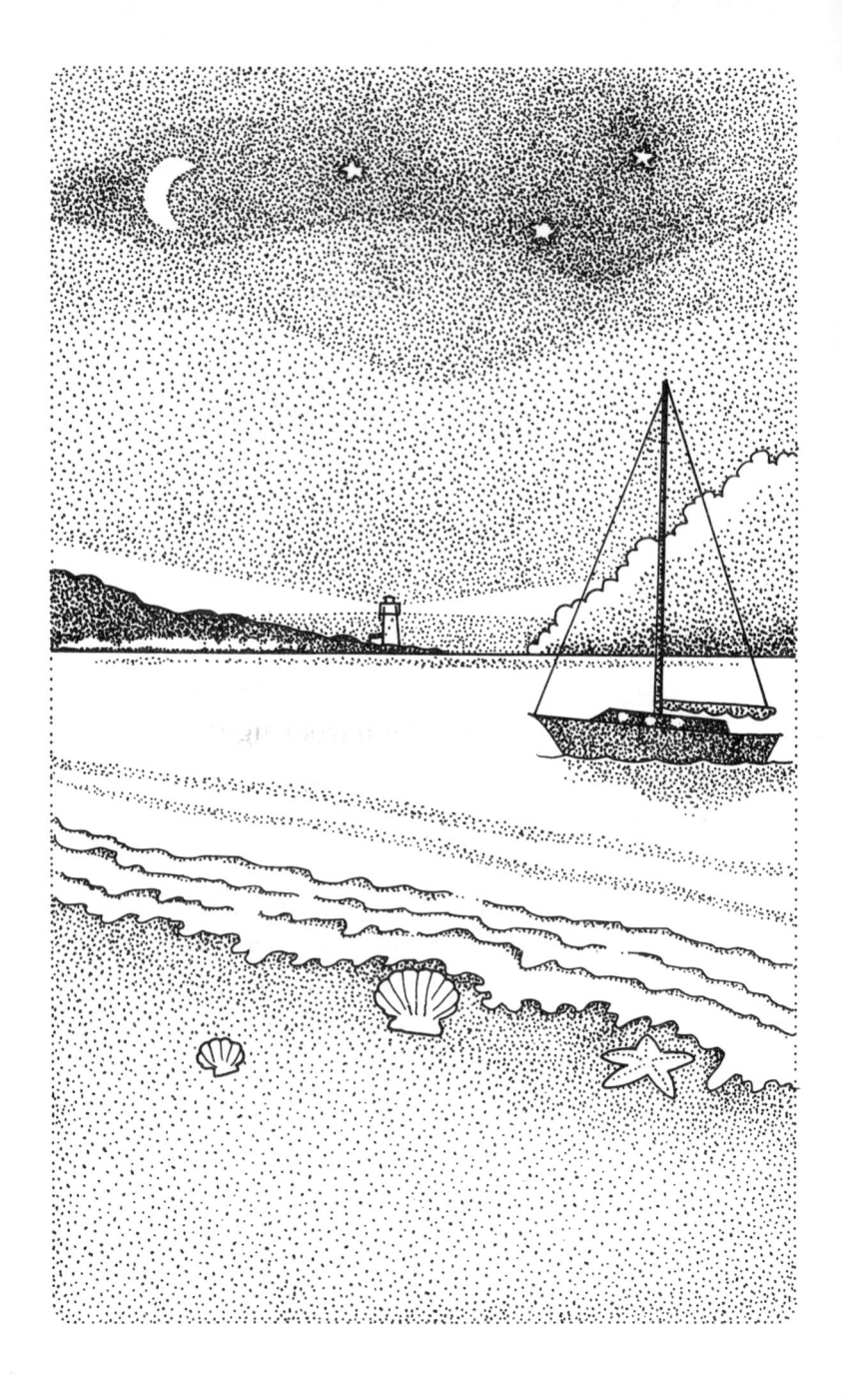

Harbor Lights

Sometimes, while still far out at sea, you can see the harbor lights. Those lights tell you that you are on course, you have made it through the storm, and your destination is in sight!

Ever since you were born, you have been on a voyage from dependence to independence. You have had your own dreams of the young woman or young man you want to become. It is a good idea to keep those dreams before you and to think of them as your own harbor lights.

With every confidence of reaching your destination, you can look forward to many a splendid day at sea!

Good seas and good sailing!

Other Youth Books from Harvest House

Katie's World Adventure Series
A new series for boys and girls

Curious, inquisitive Katie Thompsen loves adventure, loves to travel, and most of all loves to write everything in her diary. So when Katie's journalist father takes the family to faraway places, mystery and misadventure are sure to follow.

You will catch glimpses of the culture and customs of different countries and share Katie's reflections through glimpses into her secret diary. But Katie Thompsen is a special girl because she loves Jesus and loves to learn about living the Christian life.

You'll share it all as you discover this exciting new collection of books, the joy of *Katie's World*.

Katie's Swiss Adventure

Katie Sails the Nile

Katie's Russian Holiday

Katie Goes to New York

Katie and the Amazon Mystery

Katie—Lost in the South Seas

Books That Help the Hurts of Children

by Dan Quello

Each of the exciting new *Books That Help the Hurts of Children* focuses on a particular area of emotional pain or family conflict through an allegorical story written on a child's level for ages 8 through 13. The first of the 32-page books communicates understanding and hope on the problems of divorce and sibling rivalry.

CHEERING FOR THE HOME TEAM

The families that get along best think of themselves as a team. This delightful story demonstrates how much stronger family life can be when brothers and sisters move beyond competition and begin cheering for the home team!

There was nothing Scooter wanted more than to attend Judd Powers' All-Star Baseball Camp. There was nothing he wanted less than to have his kid brother, Kevin, tag along. When the plan to keep Kevin home goes terribly wrong, only one brother finds himself at camp. And then through a remarkable turn of events Kevin and Scooter find themselves on the same team!